Stuck On You

Do-It-Yourself Dating Patches for the Single Girl

Stuck On You

Do-It-Yourself Dating Patches for the Single Girl

Katie Gates and Tim Knight

Roadside Amusements
an imprint of Chamberlain Bros.
a member of Penguin Group (USA) Inc.
New York

CHAMBERLAIN BROS.
Published by the Penguin Group
Penguin Group (USA) Inc., 375 Hudson Street, New York, New York 10014, USA
Penguin Group (Canada), 10 Alcorn Avenue, Toronto, Ontario, Canada M4V
3B2 (a division of Pearson Penguin Canada Inc.)
Penguin Books Ltd, 80 Strand, London WC2R 0RL, England
Penguin Ireland, 25 St Stephen's Green, Dublin 2, Ireland (a division of
Penguin Books Ltd)
Penguin Group (Australia), 250 Camberwell Road, Camberwell, Victoria
3124, Australia
(a division of Pearson Australia Group Pty Ltd)
Penguin Books India Pvt Ltd, 11 Community Centre, Panchsheel Park, New
Delhi–110 017, India
Penguin Group (NZ), Cnr Airborne and Rosedale Roads, Albany, Auckland
1310, New Zealand
(a division of Pearson New Zealand Ltd)
Penguin Books (South Africa) (Pty) Ltd, 24 Sturdee Avenue, Rosebank,
Johannesburg 2196, South Africa

Penguin Books Ltd, Registered Offices: 80 Strand, London WC2R 0RL, England

LIBRARY OF CONGRESS CATALOGING-IN-PUBLICATION DATA
Gates, Katie.
   Stuck on you : do-it-yourself dating patches for the single girl / Katie Gates
and Tim Knight.

   p. cm.
ISBN 1-59609-058-8
   1. Dating (Social Customs) 2. Single women. I. Knight, Tim 1963- II. Title.

HQ801.G363 2005   2004061386
646.7'7'08652—dc22

Printed in China
10 9 8 7 6 5 4 3 2 1

Book design by Melissa Gerber
Cover and interior illustrations by Karen Wolcott

table of contents

Dear Single Girl,

Has your description of a dream date changed dramatically over the past few years?

· Are you impressed that he walks upright?

· Do you get excited when he has a pulse?

· Does his comb-over turn you on?

· Have you waived the language requirement?

If you answered yes to any of these questions, then you know that your dating standards have plummeted to a new low.

Maybe it's time to quit trying.

The *Stuck On You: Do-It-Yourself Dating* four-step patch process was designed to help you control these lapses in judgment. It's perfect for those times when self-help is no help at all.

Through the wonders of transdermal therapy, you'll experience all the joys of dating, without ever returning a single phone call.

It's just that easy. So relax, read on, and enjoy!

WARNING: Do-It-Yourself Dating transdermal therapy patches may cause vivid dreams, possibly featuring Antonio Banderas in a pirate suit and you in a ripped bodice. Discontinue use and start seeing a doctor *if* that doctor is single, straight, and clearly smitten with you. If pregnant or breast-feeding, what in the world are you doing trying to find a date? If not satisfied, maybe you never will be...

Congratulations!

ou've taken that first step. You realize that Mr.
Right just might not be out there. And Mr. Right
Now isn't doing the trick, either. But you don't
want to give up *all* of the feelings that come with being
in a relationship. Now, thanks to the miracle of modern
science, you don't have to.

With the transdermal *Stuck On You: Do-It-Yourself
Dating* patch system, you'll have something to go to bed
with, something to keep you warm during those long,
cold nights, something that won't roll over and go to
sleep when you want to cuddle.

There will be no more wondering how much he
really cares. In fact, this partner will be attached to you

immediately. It won't flake out. It won't be afraid of commitment. You'll never hear it say, "I need some space" or "Let's take a break."

This partner will always be sensitive to your needs and ready to take the relationship to the next level.

What you're up against: Quitting dating is hard!

Remember how exciting it was when you first started dating? It was all going to be like some Hollywood movie:

Romantic walks on the beach, the light of the full moon bouncing off the waves, perhaps with an orchestra playing your love theme faintly in the background...

Your date would have the soul of a poet and the body of a lifeguard; he would say all the right things...

And at the end of the night, when your lips touched for the first time, everything around you would fade to black...

What a crock!

Romantic walks on the beach? Sure, if you can stomach the stench of dead fish washing ashore at your feet.

Love theme? Well, if that's what you want to call a medley of car alarms, domestic disputes, and cats in heat.

If your date seems to have the soul of a poet, he's probably faking it.

If he's got the body of a lifeguard, he's probably gay.

Oh, and that kiss at the end of the night? If everything around you actually does fade to black, you should probably consult a neurologist.

Dating is *not* a Hollywood movie!

Dating is stressful, frustrating, often tedious, and sometimes dangerous.

But you have always soldiered on. If there were a Medal of Honor for bravery in the line of singles bars, you would have been weighted down with medals long ago.

Once you went AWOL from the grope and grind of happy hours and ladies' nights, you took to the information superhighway in your search for love. Internet dating seemed so promising at first. Who knew that there were so many spiritual, sexy, monogamous, and successful men available within only ten miles of your home (all for a low monthly fee)?

It sounded too good to be true, didn't it? And now, having endured fifty coffee dates in the last two months, the only second date you have is with your dentist—to get your teeth bleached.

You even let your friends set you up. That is, you *thought* they were your friends, until you met the men they claimed were perfect for you:

The Backpedalers

I'm not ready for a relationship right now ... Oh, is that my pager?

The Self-Absorbed Confessors

I love my mommy. That's why I live with her.

and the Guys with One-Track Minds.

Hey, baby, I bet you taste like the earth.

Your last date was really the clincher. It probably went something like this:

He showed up thirty minutes late, without an apology, and was talking on his cell phone when you answered the door.

At dinner, he talked incessantly about himself, chewed with his mouth open, and asked the waitress for her number.

When the bill came, he got out his Palm Pilot and calculated your share to the penny. Then, after taking your money, he charged the entire meal to his corporate credit card.

He was on his cell phone again when he slowed down the car at your corner and asked you to jump out quickly so he could make the light, shouting, "I'll call you!" as he sped away.

You don't need this!

It's time to quit.

This doesn't mean it's time to start packing for the convent. In fact, you might be taking your sexy negligee out of the mothballs very soon. You'll know when it's time. Just be patient and enjoy the four steps of the *Stuck On You: Do-It-Yourself Dating* transdermal patch process.

Getting ready

Before you start, you'll need to clear your calendar and clear your head.

Tell your girlfriends you are off the market.

The next time your mom reminds you that your clock is ticking, tell her that you've hit the snooze button.

Put away those self-help books and your tattered copy of *The Rules*.

Freeze your Internet dating memberships and cancel your subscription to the singles' series at the local museum.

Plan on being alone for a while—and loving it.

Step 1:
Anticipation

To set the mood, light some candles, put on some soft, romantic music, and open yourself to the first step: the Anticipation Patch.

Gently apply the pink heart patch to your upper arm. You may not feel an immediate change, but within the first twenty-four hours, *something* will click.

You'll giggle uncontrollably, and you'll feel more fascinating than you have in months. You might be a little tongue-tied, but you'll smile almost constantly.

Your cheeks will have a natural blush.

You'll walk with a skip in your step, and you'll have a sudden desire to kick off your shoes and jump in a fountain.

You might forget to eat, mistaking the growls in your stomach for butterflies.

You'll write poetry for the first time in years, weeping pleasurably at your deep, emotional, heartfelt verse.

After you've worn the Anticipation Patch for a few days, you'll notice that you're waiting for the phone to ring. A lot. Don't worry. This is natural. (If you don't already have a cordless, this is probably a good time to get one. Call-waiting, too.)

You may start to second-guess your emotions. This is also natural. (If you don't already keep a journal, this is probably a good time to start.)

But regardless of these worries (Is my apartment clean enough? Does this outfit make me look fat?), you'll still feel a tingly surge of anticipation. When that surge is more than you can stand, you're ready for Step 2.

Step 2:
Connection

Before applying the Connection Patch, give your legs a close shave, and get that long-overdue bikini wax.

Indulge yourself with a shopping spree at Victoria's Secret. Before you leave the mall, stop by the aromatherapy store and buy any item that includes the word "erotic" on its label.

Prepare yourself a sumptuous meal of assorted aphrodisiacs (artichokes are a must), and pour yourself a glass of wine.

Finally, drain your wineglass, throw it into the fireplace (if you don't already have a fireplace, this is probably a good time to get one), slap on the scarlet Connection Patch, and get ready for the ride of your life.

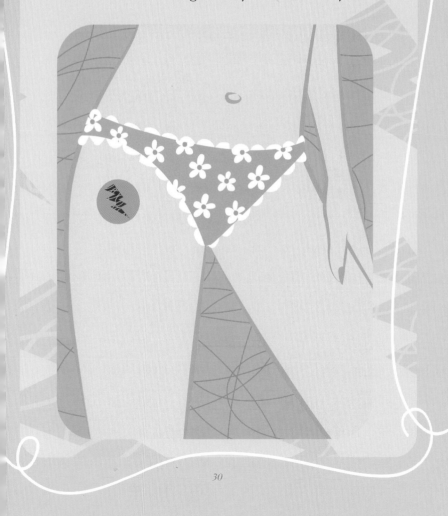

The patch will feel hot against your flesh. A delicious warmth will spread throughout your body. Don't worry. This is natural.

Your body will contort. This is also natural. (Some gentle stretching before applying the patch might be advised.)

As you writhe on your back, your heart racing, your breath short, you may call out a name ("Patch! Oh, *Patch!*"). Don't be alarmed, but don't expect a response. If you do get one, call your shrink. (And if you aren't already seeing some sort of therapist, this is probably a good time to start.)

The sensations will come in waves, intensifying until your whole body seems charged. You'll want this feeling to last forever . . . but it won't. When the surge peaks, you'll shudder and moan in satisfaction. Then you'll smile and feel utterly relaxed. (And if, afterward, you crave a cigarette—well, that's just not our problem.)

Be careful during the first few days with the scarlet Connection Patch. The surges will come frequently (and so might you), so plan accordingly. Driving on the freeway is not advised during this time. You may, on occasion, need to excuse yourself from a meeting and run to the ladies' room. But enjoy these surges, because you don't know when they will stop altogether.

By the third or fourth week with the Connection Patch, you might start to feel a little frustrated. It's becoming routine. You'll sit in office meetings wondering, "Why don't I want to jump up and leave?" You might try moving the patch to new and different erogenous zones. When you experience a brief flare, then nothing, it's time to face facts: The spark has disappeared.

When you start allowing the hair to grow back on your legs, you'll know you're ready for Step 3.

Step 3:
Commitment

After you apply the dull olive Commitment Patch, your arm might feel a little numb. Don't worry. This feeling will pass . . . to the rest of your body. This is known as the transition stage.

Now you can rest assured that you really have quit dating. If the scarlet Connection Patch felt like a roller coaster, the olive Commitment Patch will feel like a merry-go-round: pleasant, but oh so predictable.

This "ride" will make you do curious things. You'll move all your clothes to one side of the closet. You'll feel much more possessive of the remote control, at times hiding it in—where else?—remote locations. You'll complain in your journal about the chores that never get done, and your friends will look confused when you begin every sentence with "we."

Maybe you *are* acting a little strange, but you're also feeling settled. There's comfort in this patch. You don't feel like you always have to be "on." There's no pressure to impress. Nights in front of the television (once you find your remote) don't feel as lonely as they once did. You start to tackle household projects; "nesting" is no longer a dirty word.

Sometimes you think that this patch could last forever.

Then you realize that you've gained twenty pounds.

What's happened to you? If you're feeling so settled, why are you also feeling so stuck? Is prime-time TV really that good? "What happened to my sex drive?" you ask yourself, between mouthfuls of Double Dutch Rocky Road Chocolate Chip Cookie Dough ice cream. Suddenly, you're feeling trapped by the Commitment Patch, and couples' counseling isn't an option.

It's time for Step 4.

Step 4:
Reentry

Before you apply the Reentry Patch, you'll need to set the mood.

Got any Donna Summer CDs? (If not, now's a good time to get some.) Crank up "Love to Love You Baby," and apply that electric blue patch.

As you dance around your living room, feeling lighter than you have in weeks, you'll start to think about all those eligible bachelors out there.

Suddenly, the meat market never looked so inviting. Blind dates? Sure! Fix-ups? Why not! Exchanging numbers at the grocery store? Can't hurt! Prince Charming could be anywhere, and, thanks to the *Stuck On You: Do-It-Yourself Dating* patches, you've got your groove back.

Sure, you'll still have your share of misfires and disappointments, but at least you're off that damned merry-go-round. And the entire amusement park awaits.

Dating never
looked so good.

Welcome back.

Acknowledgments

We'd like to thank Laura Elizabeth Cannon for introducing us to our wonderful agent, Peter Miller. Thanks to Peter for taking a chance on the "Stuck on You Kids." Thanks to Carlo DeVito for "getting it." Thanks to editors Erin Curler and Anna Cowles, designer Melissa Gerber, and illustrator Karen Wolcott for bringing it to life. Thanks to Lynn Rosenblum for her sound advice. And back in L.A., we are indebted to our wonderful friends—Deb, Don, Julie, Naomi, Sheila, and Skipp—who provided constructive feedback and enthusiastic support.

About the Authors

Katie Gates is a freelance writer and a fundraising consultant for the nonprofit sector. She also designs jewelry and sells it through retail venues and her website.

Tim Knight is a freelance writer and editor, as well as a film critic for the website www.reel.com.. He has written and edited books on a variety of subjects. Both authors live in Los Angeles.